Wigenes Feitosa Sampaio

Business Intelligence and its application in Credit Unions

Wigenes Feitosa Sampaio

Business Intelligence and its application in Credit Unions

A study based on the BI project implemented at Sicoob

ScienciaScripts

This book is a translation from the original published under ISBN 978-613-9-63987-8.

Publisher:
Sciencia Scripts
is a trademark of
Dodo Books Indian Ocean Ltd. and OmniScriptum S.R.L publishing group

120 High Road, East Finchley, London, N2 9ED, United Kingdom
Str. Armeneasca 28/1, office 1, Chisinau MD-2012, Republic of Moldova, Europe
Printed at: see last page
ISBN: 978-620-7-72159-7

DEDICATORY

To God, for allowing me to live a blessed life full of challenges.

To my family, for always giving me all the support I needed to conquer and overcome new challenges and giving me advice that would best guide me towards achieving my goals.

ACKNOWLEDGEMENTS

To the Lord Jesus for reaching out to me with His marvellous saving grace.

To my classmates who, on a daily basis, taught me, albeit indirectly, to be a person capable of accepting differences and living with them, motivating me to take on the challenge and making me analyse and improve my practice as a learner.

To IESB for the opportunity to take this course with a faculty of the highest calibre.

To dear Professor Wanderson for all his patience, all his knowledge about credit cooperatives and *Business Intelligence, as* well as all the guidance needed to complete this work.

To my noble work colleague Mark Miranda, my mentor for this work, for all the support and transfer of knowledge passed on to me for the best quality of the content written here.

To Sicoob Confederation for the scholarship awarded to me, because through this achievement I can contribute even more to the growth of the System by applying in practice the knowledge obtained during the course.

EPIGRAPH

"I discovered that there is nothing better for man than to be happy and do good while he lives. I also discovered that being able to eat, drink and be rewarded for your labour is a gift from God." Ecclesiastes 3:12-13. New International Version (NIV).

SUMMARY

Due to the various developments that have taken place in recent years in the business world, the economic scenario has become more competitive for companies. In this context, it is necessary to make the right decisions in order to find the best direction in the market. But for this, information is considered a strategic asset and at the same time a competitive differentiator.

Information technology has proved to be a strong ally in supporting the decision-making process of organisational executives and its advances have allowed decision support systems, such as *Business Intelligence* (BI), to become indispensable solutions.

Sicoob credit unions find themselves in this same scenario. In order to be competitive in the market, these co-operatives need differentiation as a means of winning new members and retaining the loyalty of existing ones. With the implementation of a BI project at Sicoob, the cooperatives' management areas now have an analytical data environment to support decision-making.

The aim of this work is to assess the importance of the data analytics environment (BI) in decision making for leveraging business in cooperatives with a group of Sicoob professionals.

The research method used was a *survey,* with descriptive purposes, using a previously prepared questionnaire applied to 71 professionals from various Sicoob organisations.

Keywords: *Business Intelligence.* Business leverage. Credit co-operativism. Sicoob. Decision Support Systems. Information Technology.

SUMMARY

CHAPTER 1   **6**

CHAPTER 2   **10**

CHAPTER 3   **30**

CHAPTER 4   **32**

CHAPTER 5   **42**

CHAPTER 6   **45**

CHAPTER 7   **46**

CHAPTER 1

INTRODUCTION

Since the middle of the 20th century, the world has experienced major technological advances, particularly in the area of computing. These advances have led to an exponential increase in the volume of data produced. When this data is ordered and organised in a meaningful way, it forms a set called information.

Because it is considered to be the most valuable asset in a company, information has been treated differently so that its exploitation and utilisation has become an essential resource for companies seeking better results. Faced with increased competition between organisations, having quality information with a high level of reliability and relevance means having a competitive edge.

Over the years of advances in computing, Information Technology (IT) has evolved rapidly, allowing information systems to become indispensable tools for organisations, increasing the quality of the work being done and improving the organisation. The management areas of institutions began to have great opportunities in their hands to evolve in terms of the administration and management of the work provided.

A very common problem still seen today is the lack of information at the right time, inaccurate information or even incorrect information that hinders good management, as it does not make it possible to correctly analyse past data and does not help to analyse future steps.

The decision-making process requires specific information about a particular problem or situation so that the manager can analyse it and meet their needs.

To make institutional data really useful for analysis, it is important to use decision support systems (DSS). An efficient DSS allows the user to interact easily, so that they can access data and information, gaining a competitive advantage in the market in which they operate.

1.1. Theme and its delimitations

Due to the rapid and constant growth of the financial market and the aggressive competition between companies in the sector, it is crucial, and still a major challenge, for companies to offer differentiated services in the segment in which they operate. To do this, strategies must be developed to transform data into knowledge through diagnostics, analyses and data sharing, supporting managers in their perception of what is essential to the business, transforming the huge sources of information into useful, timely and reliable knowledge. Therefore, in a competitive context, knowledge is an advantage.

Therefore, knowing the company well and having well-organised and consistent information available to support decision-making is fundamental to the organisation's growth. Decision support systems, in this case, can be considered the most appropriate solution, because by collecting and consolidating the organisation's data it is possible to transform it into strategic information.

1.2. Motivation

This work was motivated by the fact that credit cooperatives are still a little explored universe in the academic world, especially in matters involving the relationship between information technology and the benefits it provides, such as support for the management of credit cooperative products and services through business management information.

1.3. Problem description

In recent years, Sicoob has experienced significant growth, both in terms of geographical coverage and financial market share. As a result, the demand for analytical credit information has grown as a way of helping business managers make decisions.

With more than 450 cooperatives using automated systems to carry out their tasks, the number of reports available is significant and most of them are static, burdening the cooperatives' transactional environment.

There are currently more than 100 types of management reports available in the modules for each product and service, all of which are static and require considerable processing time when generated. These reports do not allow for any kind of customisation or versatility according to the user's needs.

The most modern decision support systems, which allow for greater business intelligence, are highly recommended by professionals working in this area, given their robustness and high capacity for processing large volumes of data. These systems are better known as *Business Intelligence* (BI).

After the implementation of the BI Project at Sicoob, the professionals of the co-operatives who were already using their own mechanisms or solutions to generate reports and business views were faced with a new solution to support decision-making.

This raises the question of whether BI is perceived as an important decision-making tool for leveraging business in credit unions.

1.4. General objective

To assess the importance that Sicoob's professionals attach to BI in decision-making to leverage business in co-operatives.

1.4.1. Specific objectives

- To review the literature in search of a conceptual basis on BI, credit co-operativism and Sicoob;

- Describe the stages for implementing Sicoob's BI Project;

- To measure, by means of a questionnaire, the level of perception of the importance of BI in decision-making to leverage business in co-operatives.

1.5 Justifications

1.5.1 Opportunity

The opportunity to carry out this work is justified by the fact that Sicoob is interested in seeking new solutions to improve the management of services and products in co-operatives. Based on this interest, the following situations were mapped:

-Manual interference   in data availability, consistency and comprehensiveness;

-Dependence on   the IT team to create and make available databases and tools;

-Complexity and difficulty in drawing up strategic reports for decision-making in co-operatives, due to the various existing databases;

-Lack of   advanced analytical applications to support decision-making.

1.5.2 Feasibility

This work is feasible because:

-Sicoob has a BI project underway and its implementation fulfils the requirements of the strategic planning for the 2011/2013 triennium;

-Sicoob's team of professionals, both IT and business, is qualified to carry out the project;

-There are   budget resources for developing solutions and maintaining their operation;

-Sicoob has an information technology infrastructure that supports the implementation and maintenance of a specific BI environment;

-The return on investment meets the expectations of the business.

1.5.3. Relevance

This work is relevant because it will contribute to the development of the theme and further the area of knowledge related to credit cooperatives. It will also demonstrate how important BI is considered to be for credit unions as a tool for leveraging business from the perspective of Sicoob's professionals.

CHAPTER 2

THEORETICAL FRAMEWORK

2.1. *Business Intelligence* (Bi) Solutions

With the advance of information technology and information systems, the increasing use of automated systems is noticeable. The implementation of automated systems allows for a reduction in manual activities, operational errors and, above all, an increase in efficiency and optimisation of the resources involved.

For Albertin (2003, pg. 8):

> Information technology has been considered one of the most important components of today's business environment, and Brazilian organisations have made extensive and intensive use of this technology at both strategic and operational levels.

In addition to the natural systemic growth of companies, there is also an increase in data related to human collaboration, such as emails, web pages, documents, instant messaging conversations and social networks. Nowadays, this increase in data volume, which is the result of the use of information technology applications, has been exponential, since the contemporary world has become increasingly digital and is experiencing what is known as the Internet of Things[1] .

According to Oliveira (2002), information is generated all the time and in different situations. The information created by companies must be kept for future decisions whenever necessary and must be arranged in an order that meets the needs of the end user.

The variety and quantity of information produced in a company's business environment has become a key factor in the decisions to be made by executives. And for this to happen, it is important that this data is stored and analysed in order to generate information that supports decision-makers when the time comes.

According to Mattos (2005) and illustrated in Figure 1, information is generally linked to hierarchical position within the organisation and can be classified as:

-Operational Information: necessary for the operational area to obtain information from the past or present;

-Management   Information: necessary for the tactical level to obtain information on the past, present or short term;

-Executive   information: necessary for the strategic level of the organisation to obtain

---

[1] The Internet of Things is the network of physical objects accessed via the Internet, as defined by technology analysts and visionaries. Source: http://www.cisco.com/web/solutions/trends/iot/overview.html

medium and long-term information.

Figure 1 - Information hierarchy.

Source: http://campeche.inf.furb.br/empinf/empreendedor/ files PN/5200

Regardless of the hierarchical level, information will always be an important tool for both decision-making and planning at the strategic, tactical and operational levels that make up the organisational structure.

> The information generated by computer applications provides managers with a set of indicators about the business, which give them an indication of what has happened in the past and allow them to draw up scenarios for the future (SANTOS and RAMOS, 2006, pg. 6).

By analysing historical and current data, decision-makers are able to extract valuable *insights into* the business, which will serve as the basis for sound decisions aimed at achieving specific objectives or planning better results.

The business environment has become more complex because it is changing rapidly and as a result decisions have become more difficult. As a result, companies must react and adapt to changes as quickly as possible, making better decisions faster.

Based on the context described above, *Business Intelligence* (BI) solutions or systems can be applied to help improve business management, making it possible to transform data into information and information into knowledge. This makes it possible to add intelligence to organisations' businesses with greater agility and assertiveness.

According to Barbieri (2011, p. 108), BI should be understood as the development process aimed at implementing exclusive structures for information storage bases that will support the company's intelligence layer and that can be applied to its business as differential and competitive elements.

> *Business Intelligence* systems use the data available in organisations to provide relevant information for decision-making. They combine a set of tools for interrogating and exploring data with tools for generating reports to produce information that will later be used by the organisation's top management to support decision-making (SANTOS and RAMOS, 2006, p. 2).

These systems allow any type of organisation to gain a more detailed understanding of the factors that affect or could affect its business, and from there to create internal and external conditions that favour the success of its business.

In relation to BI, Turban *et al* (2008, p.47) emphasise the use of these applications:

> *Business Intelligence* is spreading its wings to embrace everyone, from small and medium-sized businesses to large organisations. Just as there are big players in BI for large corporations, there are also players in the small niches that serve medium and small companies.

According to Santos and Ramos (2006, p.2), BI systems help to increase collective intelligence, learning capacity and organisational creativity, even supporting the supply of new products and services so that the organisation can actively adapt to internal and external market challenges and opportunities.

According to Oliveira and Pereira (2008, p.2):

> BI helps organisations access synthesised information easily for decision-making. In this process, the act of transforming data into useful and meaningful information will be aimed at distributing this information to those who really need it and can make the right decisions at the right time.

BI systems are being used on a larger scale in the business world in order to provide the most relevant information for senior management to make the best decisions for their business. However, their use is not restricted to a small audience, but rather to various professionals from different sectors who benefit from the use of information.

"Today's organisations are getting more value from BI by extending information to many types of employees and thus maximising the use of existing data assets." (TURBAN et al, 2008, p. 47)

The main benefits of BI, according to a *survey* carried out by Thompson (2004), are:

- Faster and more accurate report generation (81 %);
- Better decision-making (78 per cent);
- Better customer service (56 per cent);
- Higher revenue (49%).

The results of another survey carried out by Eckerson (2003) among 510 corporations reveal that the benefits of BI in the view of the participants are:

- Time saving (61 %);
- A single version of the truth (59 per cent);
- Better strategies and plans (57 per cent);
- Better tactical decisions (56 per cent);

- More efficient processes (55%);

- Cost savings (37 per cent).

In addition, Leite (2007, p. 40 *apud* ABUKARI, 2003) lists the following benefits of BI:

a) Agility and reliability in generating information;

b) Integration and convergence of information from different departments into a single solution;

c) Possibility for decision-makers to quickly answer questions with *ad hoc* analyses,

d) Easy access to information *(user-friendly)-,*

e) Increased user motivation by switching from repetitive tasks of updating spreadsheets to analytical activities;

f) Business areas focus on higher value-added activities.

As Figure 2 illustrates, the basic architecture of a BI system basically consists of:

- Source systems (OLTP);

- The process of extracting, transforming and loading data (ETL);

- Development of *Data Marts* and/or *Data Warehouse;*

- Data is made available through reports in tables or graphs (data presentation layer).

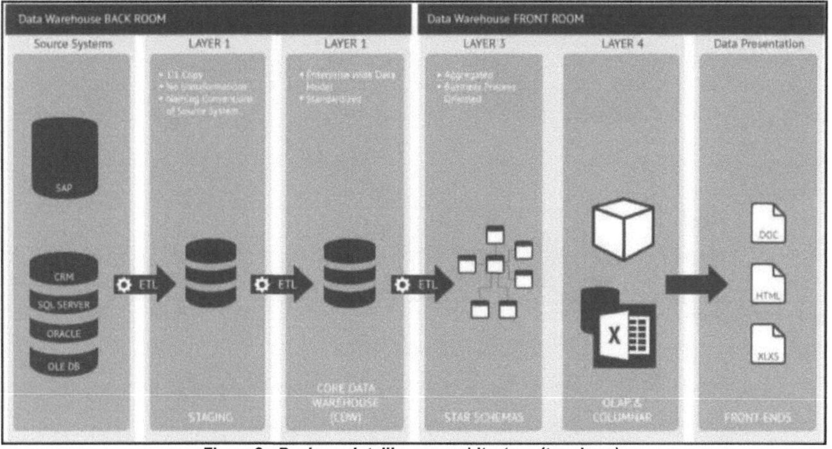

Figure 2 - *Business Intelligence* architecture *(top-down).*

Source: http://www.pmone.com/fileadmin/user_upload/pics/wiki/dw.jpg

According to Samuel Carvalho, software market analyst at IDC in Brazil *(Business Intelligence Review,* 2009, p. 6), in 2008 the *Business Intelligence* market generated around US$ 380 million in Latin America alone, approximately half of which was invested by Brazil.

The need to implement a BI solution today is not only demanded by large organisations, but also by medium-sized and even small companies. This is due to the significant increase in competitiveness in the market and in order to keep up with this evolution it is necessary to know your business better.

2.1.1. Data sources

The implementation of a BI environment in a company depends exclusively on a data source. These sources are generated by transactional systems or, as they are more commonly known, OLTP systems.

According to Kimball (2002, p. 9), OLTP systems are operational systems of record that capture company transactions and maintain a small volume of historical data.

These same systems store all the data that supports the running of an organisation's business, such as data on credit operations carried out or settled, credit card transactions, bank bill payments through self-service channels, etc. Figure 3 shows an example of an OLTP system.

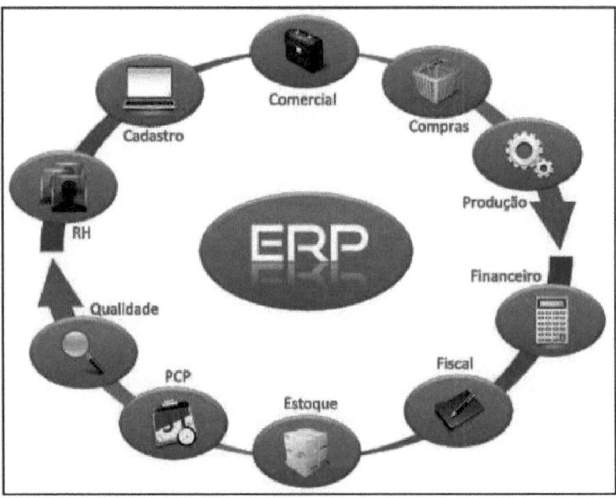

Figure 3 - OLTP system.

Source: http://www.neware.com.br/wp-content/uploads/2014/04/erp-8.png

The data in OLTP systems has a high update frequency, i.e. it is very volatile, can be modified and/or deleted and can be stored in conventional databases.

1.1.2. ETL process

ETL, or *Extract Transform and Load,* is known as one of the most critical phases in the construction of a *Data Warehouse* and/or *Data Mart.* This process is responsible for extracting, transforming and loading data, as shown in Figure 4.

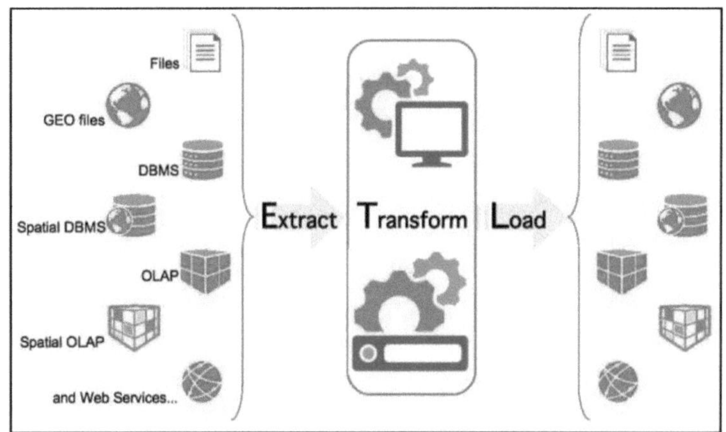

Figure 4 - ETL process.

Source: http://www.dbbest.com/blog/wp-content/uploads/2012/12/ETL input outputjpg

According to Barbieri (2011), this process constitutes the intermediate layer called *Staging* or *Staging Area,* as it is technically known, where the data will be subjected to cleaning, combining, *matching*, which will be the source of the load for the DW or DM.

Carried out using software tools, the extraction stage is responsible for collecting the data from the various sources; the transformation stage is responsible for standardising, integrating and applying rules or functions to the data collected; and the load stage is responsible for loading all the data, usually into a DW or DM in order to keep it up to date at all times, whether or not historical data is stored.

Improperly designed ETL processes can become a major problem for a BI project, as they are somewhat complex and a number of operational problems can occur.

1.1.3. *Data Warehouse*

Data Warehouse (DW) is an integrated database with a large capacity for storing data considered valuable for the decision-making process. Initially, it was intended to provide basic support to the business areas based on management information reports.

"A *Data Warehouse* is a data warehouse, an integrated repository that allows the storage of relevant information for decision making." (SANTOS and RAMOS, 2006, p. 2).

"In the early 1990s, *data warehouse* technology was proposed as a generic solution to meet organisations' need for management information." (INMON, 2005).

This repository makes it possible to analyse large volumes of data. Unlike a database in OLTP systems, the data that forms part of the DW's scope is not volatile, i.e. it doesn't change that

15

often, except when there is a need to correct data that has already been loaded.

"*Data warehouses* provide storage and maintenance capacity and can retrieve information faster than transaction-orientated databases." (ELMASRI and NAVATHE, 2005).

One of the great benefits of a DW is that it allows historical data to be stored on a much larger scale than transactional databases. A striking fact is that all the data is only available for queries, making any intervention by end users impossible.

1.1.4. *Data Mart*

The *Data Mart* is a database with a multidimensional modelling structure and essentially aims to meet the specific needs of the business areas within the company. "*Data Mart* is a database in which there is specific information for each business area (Marketing, Sales, HR or Finance)." (SILVERS, 2008).

The most simplistic definition of DM can be understood as the most specialised and specific version of a DW and its emphasis is on meeting the needs of analysis, presentation and better usability by the user in relation to a given business issue.

Just as in a DW the data comes from OLTP systems, the DM also depends on such sources. Its development is determined by the need to aggregate and organise data by business context. This makes it possible to optimise the supply of information to support decisions by focusing on the demands of an area or business process.

2.1.5. Data presentation

It refers to the set of tools that will be used by users in the organisation to navigate the DW or DM. These tools correspond to previously configured reports, applications for making reports, OLAP *(On-line Analytical Processing)* tools, *Data Mining* tools, among others. Figure 5 illustrates the ways in which data can be presented: tables, graphs and indicators.

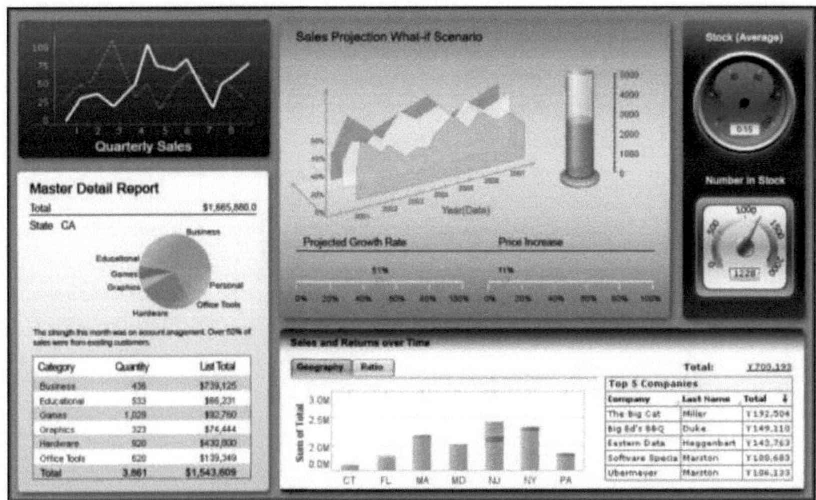

Figure 5 - Example of the data panel.

Source: http://www.inetsoft.com/images/screenshots/company dashboard.png

OLAP tools make it possible to perform some dimensional operators, which are related to the levels of detail (granularity) of the stored data. Barbieri (2011, p.103) discusses the *drill-down* and *drill-up* operators, among others. *Drill-down* is related to the operation of moving from the most summarised level of information to the most detailed, while *drill-up* is exactly the opposite.

1.1.6. *Data Warehouse* and *Data Mart* Implementation: Different Approaches

"The first *Data Warehouse* projects followed methodological paths that basically originated from two sources of inspiration: Bill Inmon and Ralph Kimball." (BARBIERI, 2011, p.112).

BI projects depend on a *data warehouse* structure that best suits the needs of the organisation. Development methodologies created by Bill Inmon[2] and Ralph Kimball[3] , considered a reference in the field, were widely used when DW structuring and construction projects began. Both Inmon and Kimball have their own approaches to DW design and construction. These approaches are known as *Top-Down* and *Bottom-Up* (see Figure 6).

---

[2] Bill Inmon is considered the father of the *Data Warehouse* concept.
[3] Ralph Kimball is considered the father of the concept of the dimensional model known as *Star Schema*.

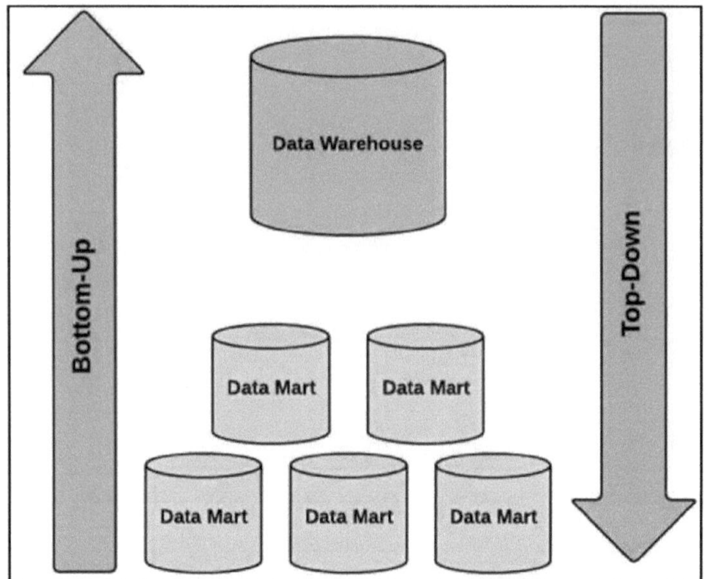

Figure 6 - *Top-Down and Bottom-Up* **approaches.**

Source: http://imagens.canaltech.com.br/54344.74448-Data-Warehouse.png

The choice of approach is a task that will depend on both your knowledge and the best application of each. Understand that the basic difference between them is the DM construction stage.

For Inmon (1996, p. 43-45), a great advocate of the *Top-Down approach* (see Figure 7), the approach to implementing a DW environment should be gradual. Over time, the first departmental or DM environments emerge. By the time it reaches a certain period of time, its architecture is largely developed.

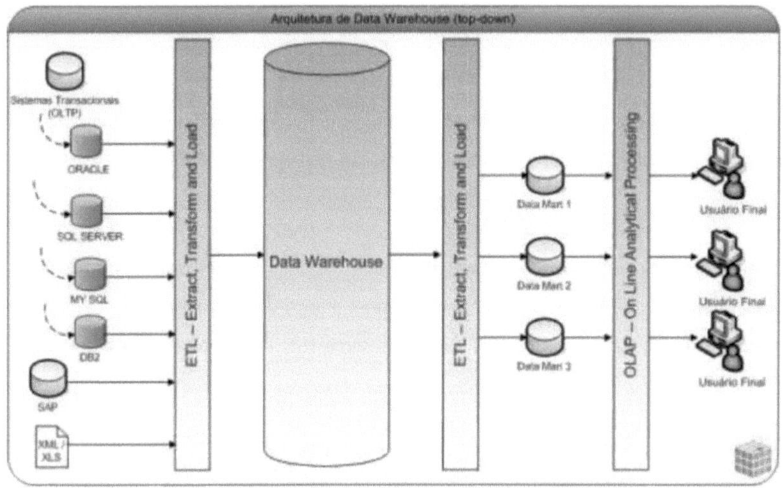

Figure 7 - DW architecture (*Top-Down* approach).

Source: http://conteudo.imasters.com.br/11321/Arquitetura BI.jpg

Inmon argues that it is more feasible to first develop a Corporate DW through modelling that integrates all the company's data, which will serve as the basis for building DMs. By creating departmental bases from a corporate base, possible incompatibilities between the data in those bases are avoided as much as possible.

In Kimball's approach, the most viable for companies is to develop several DMs, which are orientated by business issues, in order to integrate them later and thus arrive at the DW, as can be seen in Figure 8. His approach, which is very influential in the BI market, is known as *Bottom-Up.*

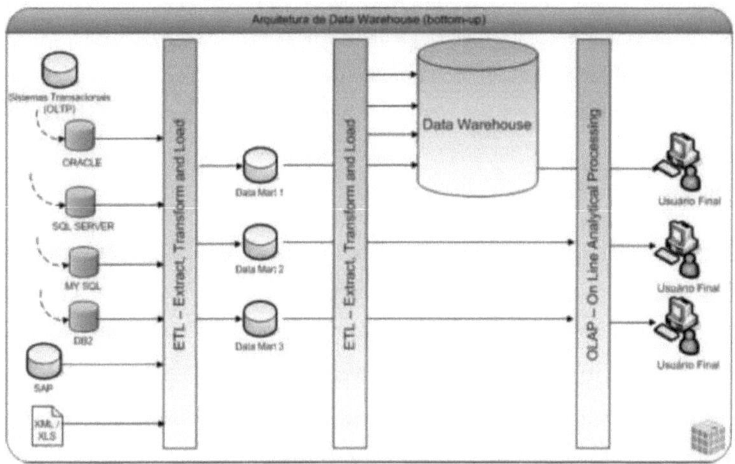

Figure 8 - DW architecture (*Bottom-Up* approach).

This model is somewhat complex, which increases the chances of failure in its implementation, as this approach depends on the corporate vision of the solution and its scope. It is only suitable for projects whose full scope is easily understood and simple to implement.

In a very objective way, understand that in the *Bottom-Up* approach, the DW derives from the integration of the DMs, while in the *Top-Down* approach, the DMs are derived from the DW. In practice, processing information in the DW is more complex due to the importance of a complete view of the organisational structure. In DM, however, it is somewhat less complex, as the focus is on one part of the business.

Another important point is that the architecture used in DW and DM is practically the same, with only a few different aspects, as shown in Table 1.

Table 1 - Main aspects of a *Data Mars Data Warehouse*.

Data Marts	Data Warehouse
Departmental level	Corporate level
High level of granularity	Low level of granularity
Small amount of historical data	Large amounts of historical data
Optimised technology for quick query access	Technology optimised for storage and management of
	large amounts of data
Each departmental area has its own specific characteristics	Structures are reconstructed for understanding at a corporate level

Despite the disagreement between Inmon and Kimball over the approaches and the differences between the aspects of each, the fact is that there is no right or wrong approach, nor the most beneficial aspect, as the best choice depends on the nature of the project and the specific needs of each business in the company. It is therefore up to each company to assess its needs and opt for the best solution.

2.1.7. Dimensional or multidimensional modelling

For Hokama *et al* (2004, p. 23), the dimensional data model emerged in order to cater for analytical processing systems used to assist in the decision-making process. These systems generally cater for a small number of users, who carry out planned queries to meet their management needs.

Decision-making, which is generally based on analytical data, needed a data model to provide greater support for the process. Thus, the so-called dimensional or multidimensional data models were created.

According to Machado (2004), multidimensional modelling is a technique for designing and visualising a data model that refers to a set of measures that describe common business aspects. Its application is particularly in summarising and restructuring data, as well as presenting it in views that support the analysis of data values.

In dimensional modelling, data is summarised and presented in a format that is easier to understand, giving greater strategic business vision. Its design and visualisation technique allows important characteristics to be perceived in the analyses, which can add greater value to the business.

According to Barbieri (2011, p. 96), data modelling is a design technique that takes data to a stage where the information is at the intersection of several dimensions. This technique is quite common in the construction of DW and/or DM, the primary objective of which is to present the data in a standardised and intuitive architecture, thus enabling high-performance access.

In practice, the biggest beneficiaries of the results of dimensional data model applications are end users in the business areas. These models not only provide a more intuitive construction of views by cross-referencing diverse data and an architecture that supports high-volume queries with shorter response times, but also make it possible to optimise the data analysis process by simplifying the presentation of the scope.

According to Barbieri (2011, p. 96), it is through dimensional modelling that the user perceives the data in a way that is close to their understanding from various perspectives.

The structure of the dimensional model is made up of fact tables and dimension tables.

2.1.7.1. Fact tables

Fact tables are considered the most important tables in dimensional data modelling, as they store data that quantifies business facts or events.

"A fact table is the main table of a dimensional model in which the numerical measurements of company performance are stored [...]" (KIMBALL and ROSS, 2002, p. 21).

All the attributes that store value, quantity or indicator of some business fact make up the measures. These measures are generally used as Key Performance Indicators (KPIs) to assess the performance of a particular business issue.

According to Barbieri (2011), a fact table contains several facts or business events, each of which can store one or more numerical measures. These measures form the dimensional analysis values. As well as recording facts that can be analysed, these tables are made up of a primary key, formed by a unique combination of dimension key values, and the metrics that are of business interest to the organisation.

In order for the values to be analysed and interpreted more easily by users, it is important that there is an intersection between the measures and the content of the dimension tables. As such, dimension tables can be considered the entry point for fact tables.

2.1.7.2. Dimension Tables

Dimension tables are the complementary tables in the dimensional model, since they store qualitative data relating to business events, as well as various attributes that describe in detail all the characteristics that define it.

In Barbieri's (2011) view, these tables represent business entities, which form the input structures that store information related to time, product, customer, etc.

It is a table that contains attributes that contextualise business event data. It qualifies the information from the Fact table. It allows data to be analysed from multiple perspectives. These attributes will be needed to aggregate and classify the facts as necessary.

Barbieri (2011) explains that dimension tables have a 1:N relationship with the fact table, which means a much smaller number of records and are the input tables for analyses, through which the user defines the parameters of their data query, i.e. they are the tables in which search filters are carried out. They have columns of information, often hierarchical, and have a primary key that must be linked to the fact table so that the two are associated.

Ideally, the attributes of the dimension tables should be filled in with intuitive values, as they are information

related to the company's business, and avoid, whenever possible, the use of unnecessary code that makes no sense to users.

2.1.8. Defining the dimensional model

When building a dimensional model, Kimball (2002, p. 36-38) systematically considers 4 (four) stages: a) selecting the business process to be modelled; b) stating the level of detail (grain) of the business process; c) choosing the dimensions that apply to each row of the fact table; d) identifying the numerical facts that will fill each row of the fact table.

In a structured and logical way, building a dimensional model is a four-stage process.

Before carrying out each stage of this process, it is necessary to consider the business requirements that will be met. These requirements are obtained through the requirements gathering process with the business areas.

"Of course, we need to consider the requirements of our business users and the reality of our source data [...] to make decisions regarding the four steps, [...]" (KIMBALL, 2002, p.38).

Generally speaking, business requirements describe in business terms what must be delivered or obtained in order to add value. A poorly designed requirements elicitation process, especially one that doesn't focus on identifying the main objectives, is highly likely to fail.

The first stage is responsible for selecting the business process to be modelled. To do this, it is essential that the business requirements are defined and their understanding aligned with the existing data in the OLTP systems, in order to meet existing needs.

In the second stage, declaring the grain is of paramount importance for modelling, as it allows the level of detail of the measurements that will make up the tables to be defined. Kimball (2002, p. 37) emphasises that this is a fundamental stage that cannot be taken lightly. In Kimball's view (2002, p. 41), the greater the detail of the factual measurements, the more information can be obtained.

In the third stage, where the dimensions that apply to each row of the fact table are chosen, it is important that the grain is defined. To do this, the dimensions must consistently represent all the descriptions needed to contextualise each numerical measure of the business process.

Identifying the numerical facts that will fill each row of the fact tables is the fourth and final stage. Here, all the measures that will be part of the fact tables will be defined. According to Kimball (2002, p. 28), the answer to the question "What are we measuring?" determines the facts or business measures that interest users. Facts with different granularities must be dealt with in specific fact tables for their level of detail.

2.1.9. Modelling techniques

Currently, the main dimensional data modelling techniques used are the *Star Schema* and the *Snowflake Schema*.

2.1.9.1. *Star Schema*

The Star *Schema* modelling technique proposes the creation of a simpler, incremental model. This model is called a star because the fact table is in the centre of the model and the dimensions are positioned around it, which refers to the shape of a star.

According to Hokama et al. (2004, p. 32-33 *apud* POE, KLAUER, BROBST, 1998), in the *Star Schema* all the dimension tables relate directly to the fact table. This sch*ema* has a simple structure, with few tables and few relationships. It resembles the business model, making it easier to understand even for end users who are not normally familiar with database structures.

Figure 9 shows the *Star Schema* model.

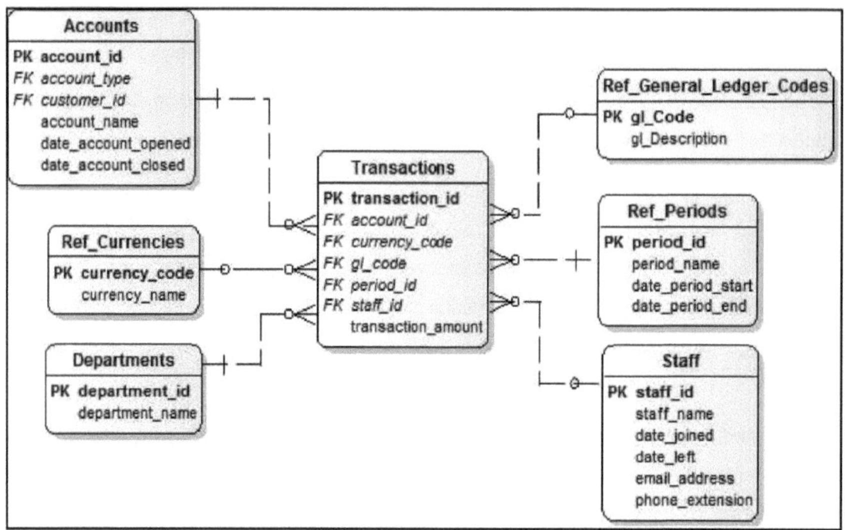

Figure 9 - Example of the *Star Schema* model.

Source: http://www.databaseanswers.org/data models/star schema/images/data model.gif

Its concept was conceived by the renowned professor Ralph Kimball, when he proposed a vision for database modelling for SAD. Its main characteristic is the presence of highly redundant data, a technique known as denormalisation, which means better performance in queries.

"The use of the star scheme is highly recommended due to the performance gain aspects when compared to the snowflake scheme." (BARBIERI, 2011, p.169).

Because it is a model that provides better performance, *Star* Schema has proved to be the most applicable in DW projects. However, like any other model, *Star Schema* has its advantages and disadvantages, as shown in Table 2.

Table 2 - Advantages and disadvantages of *Star Schema*.

Advantages	Disadvantages
Improved performance in data queries.	Denormalised tables, causing greater data redundancy.

Fewer tables in the data model.	Requires more storage space.
Simpler and easier navigation through the query tools.	

2.1.9.2. *Snowflake Schema*

According to Machado (2004), the *Snowflake Schema* model is a variant of the *Star Schema.* The main characteristic of this model, compared to the *Star Schema,* is that there is a separation of dimension hierarchies into separate tables, which derive from the main dimension.

This is the dimensional data model where, as well as relationships between dimension tables and fact tables, there can be relationships between the dimensions themselves, i.e. interconnected dimensions. It's as if each dimension had a branch. In this way, the model very much resembles a snowflake, as can be seen in Figure 10.

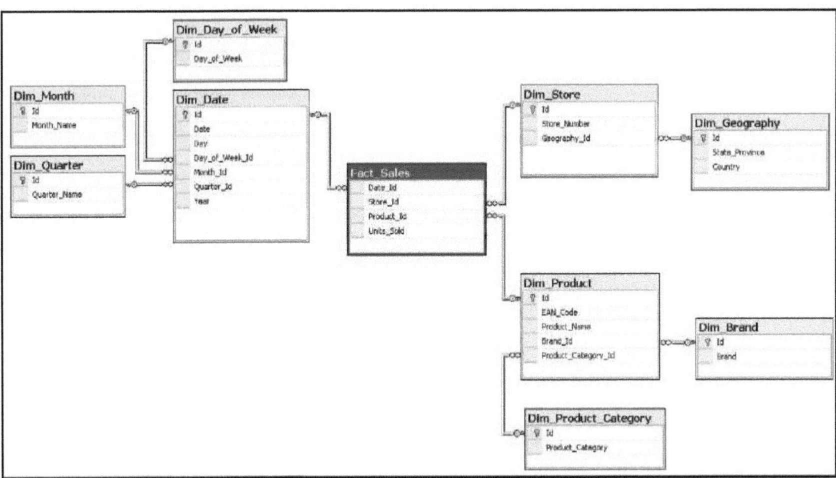

Figure 10 - Example of the *Snowflake Schema* model.

Source: http://upload.wikimedia.Org/wikipedia/commons/7/73/Snowflake-schema-example.png

The *Snowflake* model, according to Machado (2004), is the result of the third normal form or normalisation of dimension tables, thus avoiding the redundancy of textual values in a table and making existing hierarchies more visible.

The interconnection between dimensions in the snowflake model is due to the need to normalise each dimensional table in order to ensure data integrity and reduce the space occupied by these tables.

According to Machado (2004), this modelling technique can pollute the model whenever the existing dimensions increase, so that the identification of the main dimensions and their hierarchies is compromised to the point of making it difficult to visualise the data.

Snowflake Schema has not been a highly recommended model in DW projects, since its disadvantages have major negative impacts for the user, especially in terms of performance and structure complexity. Table 3 shows some important points regarding the advantages and disadvantages of this model.

Table 3 - Advantages and disadvantages of *Snowflake Schema*.

Advantages	Disadvantages
Standardised tables.	More tables in the model.
Less space for storing dimensional data.	Greater difficulty in navigating through the tools.
Greater data integrity.	Lower performance in data queries, given the complexity of the SQL generated.
	Greater complexity of the structure.

2.2. Fundamentals of Cooperativism

According to Meinen and Port (2012, p. 49), cooperativism is a socio-economic alternative with the aim of building a better life for hundreds of millions of people around the world, which makes it the largest non-governmental organisation on the planet.The International Cooperative Alliance (ICA), considered the largest association representing the cooperative movement in the world, at its congress held in the city of Manchester in England in September 1995, states that:

> A co-operative is an autonomous association of people, united voluntarily, to meet their common economic, social and cultural needs and aspirations, through a collective and democratically controlled enterprise.

On the Central Bank of Brazil's website (accessed on 16 June 2014), the concept of a credit union is: "A financial institution formed by an autonomous association of people united on a voluntary basis, with its own legal form and nature, of a civil, non-profit nature, set up to provide services to its members, the purpose of which is to provide financial services in a simpler and more advantageous way to its members, enabling access to credit and other financial products (investments, loans, financing, receiving bills, insurance, etc.)".

The Credit Cooperative Portal (accessed on 16 June 2014) defines a credit cooperative as a credit institution organised in the form of a cooperative society, maintained by the cooperative members themselves, who play the role of both owners and users.

In summary, from all the above concepts, it can be said that a credit union is a voluntary association of people with a single, non-profit objective, who are looking for better opportunities to access credit and other financial services.

It is important to note that the main objective of credit cooperatives is to provide financial services in the most accessible and simple way to their members under the most favourable conditions. Among the many advantages of setting up a credit union, perhaps the most interesting is that any surpluses or profits can be distributed among the members themselves. In order for this to happen more fairly, the assumption is that the greater the member's profitability, i.e. the greater their participation in the cooperative's positive results, the greater their share in the apportionment of these surpluses.Because they operate in more remote areas, these cooperatives are effective in strengthening the local economy, supporting the democratisation of credit and making it possible to decentralise income.

2.3.   THE BRAZILIAN CREDIT CO-OPERATIVE SYSTEM (SICOOB)

Co-operatives at national level have their own legislation, Law 5.764/71 and Complementary Law 130/2009. According to Law 4.595/64 (BRASIL, 1964), credit cooperatives are considered financial institutions in Brazil, and all authorisation to operate and supervision is the responsibility of the Central Bank of Brazil.

Under the aegis of what has been described above, the Sistema de Cooperativas de Crédito do Brasil (Sicoob), the largest credit cooperative system[4] , comes into play, operating under the following organisational model:

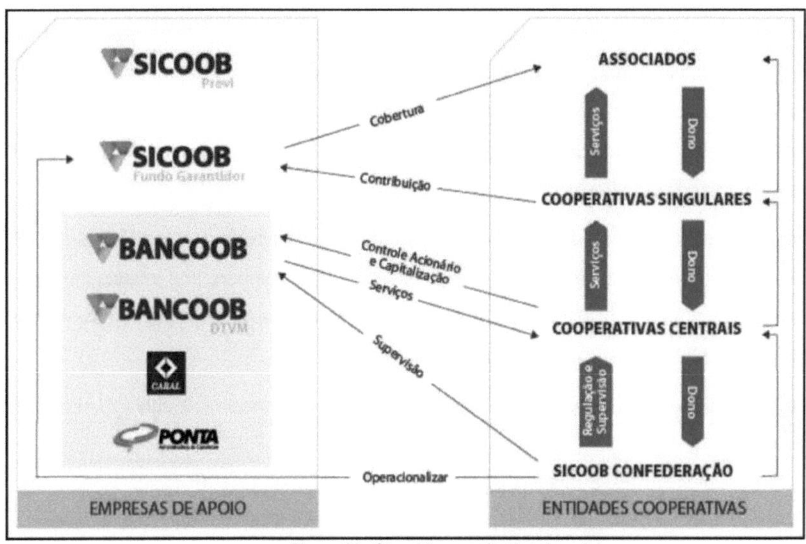

Figure 11 - Sicoob's organisational model.

Source: http://www.sicoob.com.br/modelo-organizacional

---

[4] Based on consolidated data up to Dec/2013, available at
http://cooperativismodecredito.coop.br/cenario-brasileiro/dados-consolidados-dos-sistemas-cooperativos/.

According to Figure 11 above, Sicoob is made up of co-operative entities and support companies. The co-operative entities are made up of the Confederação Nacional das Cooperativas do Sicoob Ltda - Sicoob Confederation, Banco Cooperativo do Brasil S.A.. - Bancoob, and the Central and Individual Cooperatives.

The Sicoob Confederation was set up by the Central Cooperatives with the aim of defending their interests and, above all, enabling the cooperatives to have access to technological solutions and management information services.

Bancoob, a private commercial bank controlled by Sicoob's central cooperatives, specialises in providing services to credit unions.

credit. Considered an agent that facilitates cost reduction for these co-operatives, Bancoob develops and makes available the same products and services commonly offered by other Brazilian banks.

The central co-operatives are made up of Sicoob's individual co-operatives and promote their regional and state integration. As providers of various services, they centralise the funds raised by their cooperatives and supervise the control of deposits and loans.

Single member cooperatives are financial institutions resulting from the association of people from specific economic segments, which are characterised by the direct provision of financial services to members in a simpler and more advantageous way.

With regard to support companies, Sicoob has: Bancoob DTVM, a securities distributor; Sicoob Previ, a foundation offering a supplementary pension plan; Cabal Brasil, a card brand and processor; and Ponta Administradora de Consórcios. As a way of protecting members' funds and lending credibility to the System, Sicoob's Individual Cooperatives are associated with the Credit Cooperative Guarantee Fund (FGCoop).

Not unlike traditional banks, Sicoob offers all the products and services that a traditional bank has, but in a very different way: it shares the results with its members and invests the funds raised in the communities themselves, which boosts local commerce and production as well as creating new opportunities for employment and income.

The Credit Cooperativism portal (COOPERATIVISMO, accessed on 2 July 2014) reports that:

> In Brazil, the 1,200 or so existing co-operatives manage assets of around US$ 70 billion from 6 million members. Together, the co-operatives rank 6th[a] among the largest financial institutions in the country. The main co-operative systems operating in the country are SICREDI, SICOOB, UNICRED, CONFESOL, CECRED and also independent (single) co-operatives not linked to a Confederation or Central.

Figure 12 shows the entire area covered by Sicoob in the country. The only states where the Sicoob network does not currently operate are Ceará and Roraima.

Figure 12 - Map of Sicoob's coverage.

Source: http://www.sicoob.com.br/documentsZ10180/9134021 /presença Sicoob.jpq

In its quest for better results, Sicoob has been operating under a set of characteristics, defined by its vision, mission and values. Its vision is to be recognised as the main financial institution driving the economic and social development of its members. Its mission is to generate adequate and sustainable financial solutions, through co-operativism, for its members and their communities.

Their values are based on (o):

-Transparency   ;

-Commitment   ;

-Respect   ;

-Ethics   ;

- Solidarity;
- Responsibility.

CHAPTER 3

METHODOLOGY

3.1.   Research design

This research is characterised as descriptive. According to Gil (2002, p. 42), this type of research has "[...] as its primary objective the description of the characteristics of a given population or phenomenon or the establishment of relationships between variables".

As for the research method, the *survey* was adopted, which according to Freitas *et al* (2000, p.105-106), is recommended when: the researcher intends to investigate "what", "why", "how" or "how much" a certain situation occurs, and it is not possible through the method to determine dependent and independent variables; the research takes place at the present time or recently and deals with real situations in the environment.

In this way, a *survey* is the method used to collect information with people as the target audience. This information is related to a variety of issues concerning health, beliefs, education, finances, etc.

The research deals with the largest credit cooperative system in Brazil, called Sicoob, where the Executive Board detected the need to implement an analytical environment for the data of the cooperatives affiliated to Sicoob.

The study will use data from some credit cooperatives as an example, and their names or any references that identify them or their members/clients will be de-characterised in order to maintain the confidentiality of the data.

3.2.   Data collection procedures and instruments

The research was divided into two stages: a literature review and a questionnaire.

The bibliographical review, or first stage, was carried out by reading and consulting books, magazines, websites and articles on the key themes of the work, as well as other documentary sources that the company has.

The second stage used the survey research method, recommended by Freitas et al (2000, p. 105-106), when the interest is to produce quantitative descriptions of a population and when the natural environment is the best situation to study the phenomenon of interest.

To this end, data was collected from 71 professionals who work at Sicoob Confederation, central and individual cooperatives and Bancoob and who already benefit from or use data from the analytical environment. We opted to use a questionnaire made up of 6 closed questions that aimed to capture the perception of these professionals regarding the importance of the analytical data environment (BI) in decision-making to leverage business.

Data was also collected on the characteristics of the professionals and the results showed that of the 71 interviewees, only 10 were women and 61 were men. Almost half of the respondents (46 per cent) had worked for the company for more than eight years. Those who had completed postgraduate studies (Specialisation / Master's / Doctorate / PHD) accounted for 66%, while 45% held the position of Manager / Coordinator.

CHAPTER 4

THE IMPLEMENTATION OF SICOOB'S BI PROJECT

According to Barbieri (2011, p. 117-118), one of the critical success factors is getting strong sponsorship for the BI project within the company. BI projects are generally expensive and resource-intensive.

However, the Executive Board of Sicoob Confederation, believing in the benefits that projects of this type provide, began to invest in the resources and time needed to implement this project at Sicoob, with a view to providing more intelligent decisions in the day-to-day work of co-operative managers.

In fulfilment of its purpose of providing services, supervision and operational, financial and technological integration, and based on the information needs of Sicoob's member cooperatives, Sicoob Confederação created a systemic project for BI, which was installed in July 2011.

Its main objective is to provide gains in modernisation, systemic standardisation and the development of solutions for decision-making and business intelligence, giving Sicoob's agents greater competitiveness, agility and security.

The Executive Board created a multidisciplinary team made up of members from the business and IT areas of Sicoob Confederation and Bancoob. This team also involved a consultancy specialising in analytical solutions for corporate environments, whose main activity was to identify the needs and define the objectives to be achieved with the project.

A technical committee (Cotec) was also defined, made up of 8 Central Cooperatives of the Sicoob System, each represented by 2 professionals from the business and information technology areas. This committee was tasked with defining, evaluating and monitoring the guidelines for the entire project, while maintaining alignment with Sicoob's strategic planning.

To this end, the project was structured around three pillars: Performance, Relationship Marketing and Risks and *Compliance*. This work focuses on the Performance pillar, with its scope covering data on the financial products and services of co-operatives as a whole.

In order to perfect and improve the decision-making process, providing management information with quality, precision and confidence, as well as guiding business decision-making, the entire project team engaged in the process of structuring and developing an analytical environment following the best practices for BI solutions.

3.3.   Mapping the current situation

The project's multidisciplinary team, together with the specialised consultancy, started from the premise of first mapping the situation of the cooperatives' management information environment at the time and what initiatives each had in place.

A face-to-face meeting was therefore held with the entire project team, where each Cotec member centre demonstrated which solutions were already being used for decision-making in their corporate environment. With the information presented at the meeting, the contracted consultancy began to consolidate the main points discovered.

Among the points mapped, the following findings stand out:

a) Although there are mechanisms in place to feed data from Sicoob Confederation into the Individual Cooperatives' BI, there are considerations regarding access and limitations on the availability of data.

b) Lack of unity in corporate visions and standardisation of key performance indicators;

c) Although there are BI systems in each Individual Cooperative, the production of reports is not efficient and is limited to command and control actions, without advanced simulation and analysis views;

d) BI tools with limitations in use and access;

e) In-house development of BI solutions and tools;

f) Need for additional development for each planning and simulation requirement, both in data extraction (Sicoob Confederation) and in the presentation layer (in Central and Individual Cooperatives);

g) Although BI and CRM systems exist in some co-operatives, there is a lack of a single view of the customer;

h) Information used in reports and analysis panels, but not integrated into business processes;

i) High data preparation effort, compared to low productivity and meeting users' analysis needs;

j) Dependence on IT to create and make available databases and tools, but with some difficulty in providing the various analytical views required by the business;

k) Data quality problems arising from divergent concepts of performance indicators;

l) Difficulty for Central and Individual Cooperatives in integrating internal data with data from the Sicoob Confederation, since Central and Individual Cooperatives create their own bases for their analyses, defining their own rules for integration and generation of indicators.

Based on these points, the first requirements gathering meetings were held with the Central and Individual Cooperatives and the business managers of both Sicoob Confederation and Bancoob.

The expectation of all the managers is that the analyses of the data will make it possible to obtain and structure them at different levels of detail, which are related to:

a)   Information on service centres (PA);

b)   Information from managers;

c)   Membership information.

Another crucial step is to hold business understanding meetings between the business team and the TL team. These meetings are important because they provide the best opportunity for the IT team,

responsible for building the analytical data scope, to understand the business's information needs more clearly.

To this end, a map of understanding was created, containing all the requirements and their respective business rules. The clarifications cover both business concepts and calculation details, where applicable, so that the database meets the needs raised.

After liaising with the business area and in possession of the map of understanding, the IT team begins the process of building the dimensional model, according to the steps described above.

If any limitation is identified in the data source that makes it impossible to fulfil one or more requirements, a document is drawn up containing all the impacts of the requirements, with each impact being technically justified.

3.4.   Approach and dimensional modelling used

The approach best suited to the project's needs is directly related to the time it takes to deliver the solution to the business. To this end, only one approach best suited the proposal to deliver the solution in a short space of time, the *Bottom-up* approach.

For its implementation, the proposal was to create independent DMs, which will take less time to develop as they only deal with one business context. In addition, the scope will contain the greatest level of detail, something that the DM has as an advantage.

In order to reduce data extraction time and speed up analysis, it was crucial that the modelling technique met these needs. The decision was therefore made to create the dimensional model using the *Star Schema* modelling technique.

Thus, the model developed can be exemplified as shown in Figure 13.

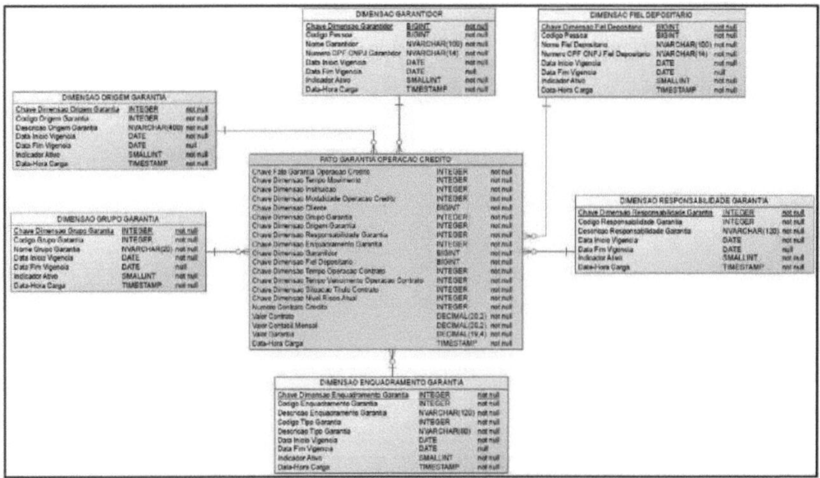

Figure 13 - Example of the dimensional model developed.

4.3   Data source and ETL processes

All the data to be extracted comes from the modules that make up the Sicoob Information Technology System (Sisbr), which stores transactional data in various databases. Most of the legacy databases are on the Microsoft SQL *Server* platform, but many have already been migrated to the IBM DB2 platform.

The ETL processes used include the extraction, transformation and loading of data from these to the *Staging Area* tables, technically called DWS by the IT department, where they are subjected to a process of standardisation and data quality treatment, and from these to the Fact and Dimension tables. The set of processes can be summarised and illustrated as shown in Figure 14 below.

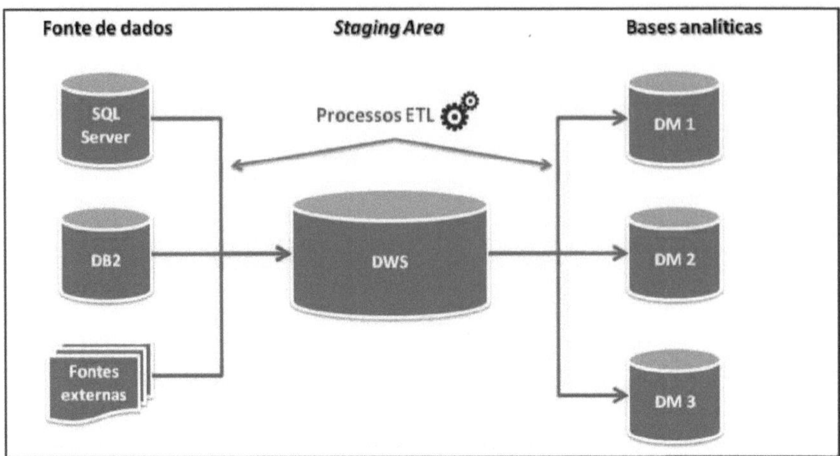

Figure 14 - ETL processes used.

Almost all of the processes run daily, with the exception of a few processes that run monthly. In order to maintain the history and facilitate data recovery in the event of a problem during the execution of these processes, all the Fact and Dimension tables have load versioning attributes.

4.4 Data consultation and presentation tool (Olap)

With the dimensional model ready and loaded, the only thing left to do was to define the tool for querying and presenting the data, i.e. the OLAP tool. This stage was fundamental in the DM implementation process, because the end user is the most interested and benefited, and for them the presentation of and access to the data should be more intuitive and user-friendly.

To this end, Sicoob conducted market research and evaluated the tools and solutions that would best meet user expectations. During the research, the magic quadrant for available BI solutions and analytical platforms was analysed on the Gartner website, as shown in Figure 15.

Figura 15 - Magic Quadrant for *Business Intelligence* platforms.

Source: Gartner. January 2011.

It is noticeable that in 2011, the solutions that proved most relevant in the market are highlighted in the *Leaders* quadrant, among which IBM, MicroStrategy and Oracle have the best acceptance. IBM provides the OLAP tool known as Cognos *Business Intelligence,* MicroStrategy provides MicroStrategy *Analytics* and Oracle has OBIEE.

In order to better explore the market tools as well as to assess which would perform best in the environment, the project team applied a proof of concept (PoC) with the main companies ranked in Gartner's *Leaders* quadrant.

The technological architecture at the time and the results obtained through PoC, which are related to high performance and easier integration into the environment, were the deciding factors for the team to acquire the OLAP tool best suited to the project.

Once integrated into the environment and available in production, the tool was used to generate reports and create *dashboards.* These *dashboards* were idealised by the business team based on the most strategic visions of each product and the prototypes were taken to Cotec for approval.

Once the prototypes had been approved, the *dashboard* development stage began, all written in detail by the project's business team and validated by the business managers.

Starting with the practicality of the OLAP tool, its use is the most effective way of measuring the applicability of the BL project. Reports with specific views of the credit portfolio will be demonstrated, comprising management analyses aimed at generating business from the data made available.

Figure 16 shows, as an example, an analytical report generated from the Monthly Contract fact table in the Credit Portfolio.

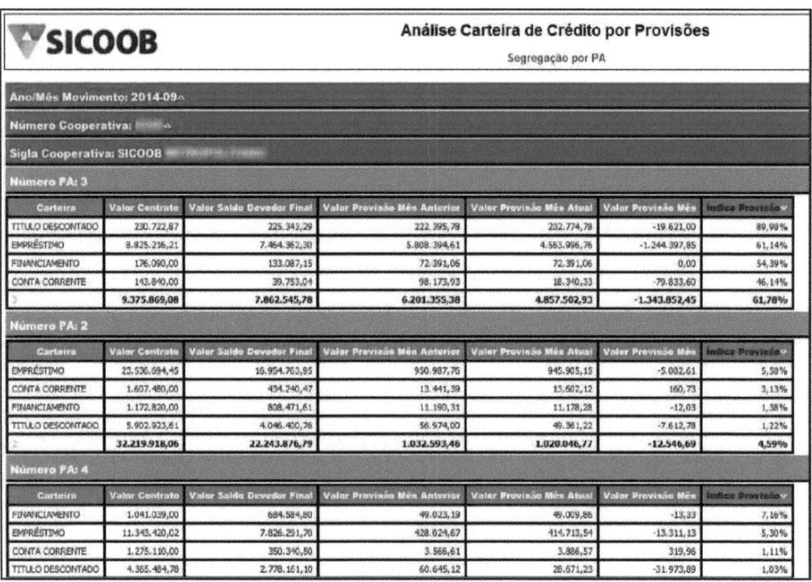

Análise Carteira de Crédito por Provisões

Segregação por PA

Ano/Mês Movimento: 2014-09

Número Cooperativa:

Sigla Cooperativa: SICOOB

Número PA: 3

Carteira	Valor Contrato	Valor Saldo Devedor Final	Valor Provisão Mês Anterior	Valor Provisão Mês Atual	Valor Provisão Mês	Índice Provisão
TITULO DESCONTADO	230.722,87	225.343,29	222.395,78	202.774,78	-19.621,00	89,98%
EMPRÉSTIMO	8.825.216,21	7.464.362,30	5.808.394,61	4.563.996,76	-1.244.397,85	61,14%
FINANCIAMENTO	176.090,00	133.087,15	72.391,06	72.391,06	0,00	54,39%
CONTA CORRENTE	143.840,00	39.753,04	98.173,93	18.340,33	-79.833,60	46,14%
3	9.375.869,08	7.862.545,78	6.201.355,38	4.857.502,93	-1.343.852,45	61,78%

Número PA: 2

Carteira	Valor Contrato	Valor Saldo Devedor Final	Valor Provisão Mês Anterior	Valor Provisão Mês Atual	Valor Provisão Mês	Índice Provisão
EMPRÉSTIMO	23.536.994,45	16.954.763,95	950.987,76	945.905,15	-5.082,61	5,58%
CONTA CORRENTE	1.607.480,00	434.240,47	13.441,39	13.602,12	160,73	3,13%
FINANCIAMENTO	1.172.820,00	808.471,61	11.190,31	11.178,28	-12,03	1,38%
TITULO DESCONTADO	5.902.923,61	4.046.400,76	56.974,00	49.361,22	-7.612,78	1,22%
2	32.219.918,06	22.243.876,79	1.032.593,46	1.020.046,77	-12.546,69	4,59%

Número PA: 4

Carteira	Valor Contrato	Valor Saldo Devedor Final	Valor Provisão Mês Anterior	Valor Provisão Mês Atual	Valor Provisão Mês	Índice Provisão
FINANCIAMENTO	1.041.039,00	684.584,80	49.023,19	49.009,86	-13,33	7,18%
EMPRÉSTIMO	11.343.420,02	7.826.291,70	428.024,67	414.713,54	-13.311,13	5,30%
CONTA CORRENTE	1.275.110,00	350.340,50	3.566,61	3.886,57	319,96	1,11%
TITULO DESCONTADO	4.365.484,78	2.778.161,10	60.645,12	28.671,23	-31.973,89	1,03%

Figure 16 - Analysis of loan portfolio provisions by AP.

Source: Sicoob's analytical environment.

Through this report, it is possible to monitor the portfolio's performance in relation to provision indices, identifying which AP contributed the most to the cooperative's results in September 2014. In this way, managers can identify assertive improvement actions.

Analysing the data in the report, it is clear that the provision ratios for PA 3 represent 61.78% of the cooperative's total ratios in the period under analysis. In other words, PA 3 is having a greater negative impact on your co-operative's results.

As for the loan portfolio performance report (see Figure 17), managers can analyse how representative the outstanding balance, grouped by individual and legal entity, of a given AP is in relation to the total portfolio during the analysis period.

		CRÉDITO RURAL		EMPRÉSTIMO		FINANCIAMENTO		TITULO DESCONTADO		Resumo	
		Crédito	%	Crédito	%	Crédito	%	Crédito	%	Crédito	%
1	PF	127.411.174,23	6,21%	78.677.952,23	3,84%	14.086.519,75	0,69%	4.360.618,55	0,21%	224.536.264,76	10,95%
	PJ	5.049.988,45	0,25%	16.646.630,08	0,81%	2.240.903,71	0,11%	2.566.906,70	0,13%	26.504.428,94	1,29%
1		132.461.162,68	6,46%	95.324.582,31	4,65%	16.327.423,46	0,80%	6.927.525,25	0,34%	251.040.693,70	12,24%
2	PF	14.490.299,02	0,71%	1.851.170,89	0,09%	1.934.244,11	0,09%	523.949,78	0,03%	18.799.663,80	0,92%
	PJ	472.765,12	0,02%	479.051,64	0,02%	586.300,65	0,03%	348.058,88	0,02%	1.886.176,29	0,09%
2		14.963.064,14	0,73%	2.330.222,53	0,11%	2.520.544,76	0,12%	872.008,66	0,04%	20.685.840,09	1,01%
3	PF	16.957.468,53	0,83%	1.621.464,34	0,08%	2.784.794,05	0,14%	435.421,81	0,02%	21.799.148,73	1,06%
	PJ			871,90	0,00%	214.994,58	0,01%	260.224,41	0,01%	476.090,89	0,02%
3		16.957.468,53	0,83%	1.622.336,24	0,08%	2.999.788,63	0,15%	695.646,22	0,03%	22.275.239,62	1,09%
4	PF	20.889.610,18	1,02%	6.700.433,88	0,33%	3.305.157,73	0,16%	935.000,87	0,05%	31.830.202,66	1,55%
	PJ			373.122,87	0,02%	1.625.515,38	0,08%	2.117.108,97	0,10%	4.115.747,22	0,20%
4		20.889.610,18	1,02%	7.073.556,75	0,34%	4.930.673,11	0,24%	3.052.109,84	0,15%	35.945.949,88	1,75%
5	PF	18.852.932,14	0,92%	2.688.654,08	0,13%	3.033.099,47	0,15%	1.054.086,76	0,05%	25.628.772,45	1,25%
	PJ			14.670.625,84	0,72%	68.144,26	0,00%	63.099,27	0,00%	14.801.869,37	0,72%
5		18.852.932,14	0,92%	17.359.279,92	0,85%	3.101.243,73	0,15%	1.117.186,03	0,05%	40.430.641,82	1,97%
6	PF	29.880.069,34	1,46%	19.533.462,21	0,95%	3.084.534,52	0,15%	71.825,50	0,00%	52.569.891,57	2,56%
	PJ			1.400.914,71	0,07%	172.433,50	0,01%	102.700,84	0,00%	1.676.049,05	0,08%
6		29.880.069,34	1,46%	20.934.376,92	1,02%	3.256.968,02	0,16%	174.526,34	0,01%	54.245.940,62	2,65%
7	PF	63.331.707,45	3,09%	11.904.214,55	0,58%	3.286.928,81	0,16%	414.470,33	0,02%	78.937.321,14	3,85%
	PJ			107.967,83	0,01%	267.691,60	0,01%			375.659,43	0,02%
7		63.331.707,45	3,09%	12.012.182,38	0,59%	3.554.620,41	0,17%	414.470,33	0,02%	79.312.980,57	3,87%

Figure 17 - Loan portfolio performance report by AP.

Source: Sicoob's analytical environment.

From a more analytical point of view, the report on reciprocity in the credit portfolio by member details the outstanding balances for each product, segregated by individual and corporate clients, and also provides the respective telephone numbers for possible contact with the member, as shown in Figure 18.

		CRÉDITO RURAL		EMPRÉSTIMO		FINANCIAMENTO		CONTA CORRENTE		TÍTULO DESCONTADO		Resumo	
		CRÉDITO	%	CRÉDITO	%	CRÉDITO	%	CRÉDITO	%	CRÉDITO	%	CRÉDITO	%
OLGA		65.753,77	0,03%	16.131.610,89	6,99%	19.027,31	0,01%	543.345,21	0,24%			16.759.737,18	7,26%
		65.753,77	0,03%	16.131.610,80	6,99%	19.027,31	0,01%	543.345,21	0,24%			16.759.737,18	7,26%
RIAD		530.755,55	0,23%	13.017.580,88	5,64%			402,22	0,03%			13.548.738,45	5,87%
		530.755,55	0,23%	13.017.580,68	5,64%			402,22	0,00%			13.548.738,45	5,87%
XPSE		12.048.605,14	5,22%					0,00	0,00%			12.048.605,14	5,22%
		12.048.605,14	5,22%					0,00	0,00%			12.048.605,14	5,22%
JOSÉ		4.773.425,12	2,07%	0,00	0,00%	2.610.530,55	1,13%	10.492,14	0,00%	4.743,26	0,00%	7.399.191,07	3,21%
		4.773.425,12	2,07%	0,00	0,00%	2.610.530,55	1,13%	10.492,14	0,00%	4.743,26	0,00%	7.399.191,07	3,21%
VICENTE		3.045.452,12	1,32%	0,00	0,00%			0,00	0,00%	2.296.120,59	0,99%	5.341.572,71	2,31%
		3.045.452,12	1,32%	0,00	0,00%			0,00	0,00%	2.296.120,59	0,99%	5.341.572,71	2,31%
OTTO		4.165.603,56	1,80%	11.636,86	0,00%			1.114.859,56	0,48%			5.292.099,98	2,29%
		4.165.603,56	1,80%	11.636,86	0,00%			1.114.859,56	0,48%			5.292.099,98	2,29%
REYNALDO		4.358.858,96	1,89%					22.180,25	0,01%			4.381.039,21	1,90%
		4.358.858,96	1,89%					22.180,25	0,01%			4.381.039,21	1,90%
IVAN		300.755,09	0,13%	4.035.596,44	1,75%			0,00	0,00%			4.336.351,53	1,88%
		300.755,09	0,13%	4.035.596,44	1,75%			0,00	0,00%			4.336.351,53	1,88%
MARCOS		764.902,43	0,33%	3.330.351,70	1,44%			0,00	0,00%	23.912,55	0,01%	4.119.166,68	1,78%
		764.902,43	0,33%	3.330.351,70	1,44%			0,00	0,00%	23.912,55	0,01%	4.119.166,68	1,78%
MARCELO		3.924.969,47	1,70%					0,00	0,00%			3.924.969,47	1,78%

Figure 18 - Loan portfolio performance report by member.

Source: Sicoob's analytical environment.

Figure 19 shows an overview of the management results related to the expenses and income generated by Sicoob's bank collection fees in September 2014.

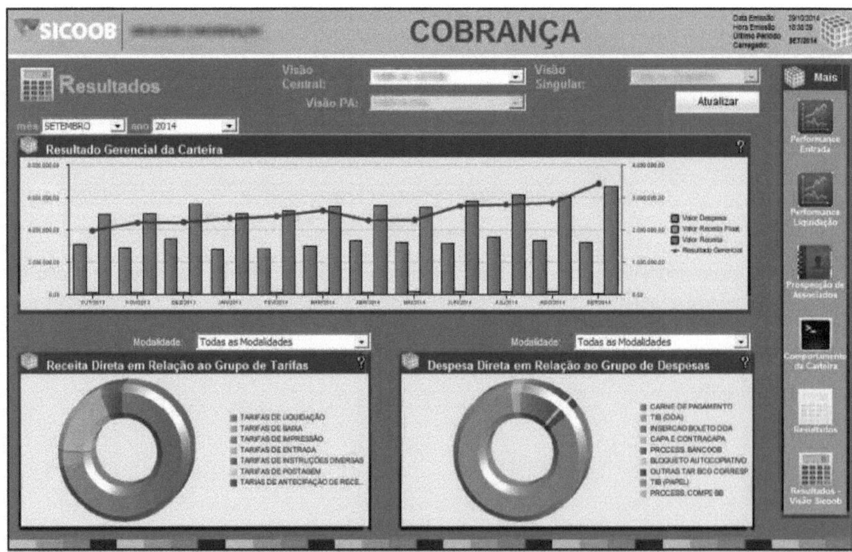

Figure 19 - Sicoob Bank Collection Results Panel.

Source: Sicoob's Analytical Environment.

Analysing the graphs, it is possible to see that the tariffs that generated the most income in the period under analysis were related to the settlement of boletos at the cooperatives, while those that generated the most expenses at the cooperative in the same period were related to interbank transfers (TIB) of boletos settlement amounts.

From the above examples, it can be seen that the implementation of Sicoob's BI Project gives co-operative managers a managerial view of each financial product and/or service. Notwithstanding this, it is also possible to monitor the financial behaviour of their members/customers in the cooperative.

CHAPTER 5

ANALYSING THE RESULTS

5.1.   Survey to assess the perceived importance of the analytical data environment (BI)

This stage shows what the professionals at Sicoob's organisations consider important with regard to the analytical data environment (BI) as a support for product and service management. Six questions were drawn up relating to the relevance of the perceptions obtained after contacting and using analytical data for Sicoob's products and services.

Each of the 71 professionals had the option of evaluating whether they agree, partially agree or disagree with each perception of the importance of the analytical data environment in decision-making to leverage business. Based on the answers, the level of importance attributed by the professionals can be seen.

Table 4 shows the number of responses for each evaluation in their respective perception, as well as the level of agreement given by the respondents.

Table 4 - Level of importance attributed to the analytical data environment.

Perception	Agree (per cent)	Partially agree (percentage)	Disagree (per cent)	Total (per cent)
1 - Access to the analytical environment allows business managers greater autonomy in analysing and obtaining results	64 (90,14%)	7 (9,86%)	0 (0%)	71 (100%)
2 - Analytical data allows managers to prospect for new business	63 (88,73%)	8 (11,27%)	0 (0%)	71 (100%)
3 - There has been a reduction in the process of extracting data to generate reports. product and service performance	45 (63,38%)	23 (32,39%)	3 (4,23%)	71 (100%)
4 - The frequency with	56 (78,87%)	14 (19,72%)	1 (1,41%)	71 (100%)

which analytical data is made available provides impr ovements in business management process			
5 - The analytical data made available provides a strat egic vision of the business	62 (87,32%)	7 (9,86%)	2 (2,82%)	71 (100%)
6-As implementations in the permiti rouma analytical environment integrated customer vision	65 (91,55%)	6 (8,45%)	0 (0%)	71 (100%)
Total (per cent)	**355 (83,33%)**	**65 (15,26%)**	**6 (1,41%)**	**426 (100%)**

Source: Research data.

In general, the results are in line with the recommendations found in the literature, with the majority agreeing (83.33%) and partially agreeing (15.26%) that BI is relevant for leveraging business in credit unions. Only 1.41 per cent marked that they disagreed with three elements related to the reduction in the data extraction process and the frequency with which data is made available, pointed out in questions 3, 4 and 5.

It is clear that the professionals interviewed attach significant importance to an integrated view of customers through implementation in the analytical environment (question 6). The majority, 92.54 per cent, agree and a further 7.46 per cent partially agree. This high level of agreement reflects the latent need to better serve customers by having an overview of their relationship with the co-operative.

Another finding is the agreement rate (90.14% agree) for question 1, where access to the analytical environment allows business managers greater autonomy in analysing and obtaining results. This indicates that the item mapped at the start of the project regarding the dependence of the business area on obtaining data from the IT team has been significantly reduced.

Question 2 assesses whether analytical data allows managers to prospect for new business. Of all the respondents, 88.73 per cent agreed, while 11.27 per cent partially agreed.

Question 5 asked whether the analytical data provided allows for a strategic vision of the business. The result of 2.82% of respondents who disagreed pales in comparison to the 87.32% who agreed, but it does cause some concern, since having a strategic vision is important for co-operatives.

Of the total disagreements, question 3 has the highest rate, corresponding to 4.23%, a situation that suggests a more detailed analysis of the main motivator. However, more than half agree that there has been a reduction in the data extraction process for generating product and service performance reports.

With regard to the availability of analytical data, as described in question 4, 78.87% agree that the frequency with which data is made available improves the business management process. Only 1.41 per cent do not agree, something that may have been motivated by the need for a period of time closer to *real-time.*

The evaluations that have answers in the "Disagree" option show a divergence between the perception of some professionals at Sicoob's organisations and what the literature recommends, but the vast majority are in line with the theoretical thoughts and recommendations.

CHAPTER 6

CONCLUSIONS

The aim of this study was to describe the implementation of the BI project at Sicoob, as well as to assess the perceived importance of the analytical data environment (BI) in decision-making to leverage business in cooperatives, among a group of 71 Sicoob professionals.

Through the literature review on the subject, it was possible to see that BI systems are indicated as an important tool in the decision-making process in the corporate environment, including for credit unions.

When analysing the data collected from Sicoob's professionals, it is possible to see that, in general, the results are in line with the recommendations found in the literature, with the majority of respondents, a total of 83.33%, agreeing that BI is relevant for leveraging business in credit unions.

Of the questions addressed, the most relevant is related to the perception that the implementations in the analytical environment will allow for an integrated view of customers (question 6), with a 91.55% "Agree" index and 8.45% "Partially agree".

Only 1.41 per cent answered "Disagree" to three elements related to the reduction in the data extraction process and the frequency with which data is made available, pointed out in questions 3, 4 and 5, which demonstrates a misconception on the part of some professionals about the benefits of BI systems highlighted in the literature.

As a result, the propositions were confirmed, pointing to the importance of the data analytics environment (BI) in decision-making to leverage business in co-operatives.

Taking into account the importance of the subject and the results obtained in this work, it is suggested that future studies be carried out into how the application of *data* mining techniques in the environment can be used in the future.

Sicoob's analytics can help its member co-operatives leverage new business.

CHAPTER 7

REFERENCES

ALBERTIN, A. L. **Management Approach to the Benefits and Challenges of Information Technology for Business Performance.** Research project developed with the support of the Research and Publication Centre (NPP) of the São Paulo Business School (EAESP) of the Getúlio Vargas Foundation (FGV). São Paulo: FGV-EAESP, 2003. Available at :< http://bibliotecadigital.fgv.br/dspace/bitstream/handle/10438/3089/P00319_1.pdf7seq uence=1>. Accessed on: 25 August 2014.

CENTRAL BANK OF BRAZIL. FAQ - Credit unions. Available at: <http://www.bcb.gov.br/Pre/bc_atende/port/coop.asp#1>. Accessed on: 16 June 2014.

BARBIERI, Carlos. **BI2 - Business Intelligence: Modelling and quality. Credit Cooperatives yesterday, today and tomorrow.** Rio de Janeiro: Elsevier, 2011.

BONOMA, T. V. **Case research in marketing: opportunities, problems and a process.** *Journal of Marketing Research,* v. 22, p. 199-208, May 1985.

BRAZIL. Law No. 4.595, of 31 December 1964. Provides for Monetary, Banking and Credit Policy and Institutions, Creates the National Monetary Council and makes other provisions. Available at :< http://www.planalto.gov.br/ccivil_03/leis/L4595compilado.htm>. Accessed on: 3 July 2014.

ECKERSON, W. **Smart Companies in the 21st Century: The Secrets of Creating Successful Business Intelligent Solutions.** Seattle: The Data Warehousing Institute, July 21, 2003. Available at :< http ://down load .101 com. com/td wi/research_re port/2003BI Report_v7. pdf >. Accessed on 28 October 2014.

ELMASRI, Ramez; NAVATHE, Shamkant B. **Sistemas de banco de dados.** 4 ed. São Paulo: Pearson Addison Wesley, 2005.

FREITAS, H.; OLIVEIRA, M.; SACCOL, A. Z.; MASCAROLA, J. The *survey* research method. **Revista de Administração,** São Paulo, v.35, n. 3, p. 105-112, July/September, 2000.

GIL, Antonio Carlos. **How to prepare research projects.** 4 ed. São Paulo: Atlas, 2002.

GARTNER, Inc. **Magic Quadrant for Business Intelligence and Analytics Platforms.** Available at: <http://www.gartner.com/technology/reprints.do?id=1- 1QYL23J&ct=140220&st=sb>. Accessed on: 5 July 2014.

HOKAMA, Daniele Del Bianco et al. **Data modelling in the data warehouse environment.** São Paulo: 2004. 120 p. Interdisciplinary Undergraduate Programme (Bachelor's Degree in Information Systems) Faculty of Computing and Informatics, Mackenzie Presbyterian University, 2004. Available at: < http://meusite.mackenzie.com.br/rogerio/tgi/2004ModelagemDW.pdf>. Accessed on: 18 August 2014.

INMON, William H. **Building the data warehouse.** 4th ed. John Wiley & Sons, 2005.

. **Building the data warehouse.** New York: Wiley Computer Pub., 1996. 401 p.

KIMBALL, Ralph; ROSS, Margy. **The Data Warehouse Toolkit: A complete guide to dimensional modelling.** Translation: Ana Beatriz Tavares, Daniela Lacerda. 2 ed. Rio de Janeiro: Campus, 2002. Original title: The Data Warehouse Toolkit: the complete guide to dimensional modelling.

LAZZARINI, S. G. **Case study: applicability and limitations of the method for research purposes.** Economia & Empresa, v. 2, n. 4, p. 17-26, October/December 1995.

LEITE, Fabiano Luiz Caídas. **Using Business Intelligence to Manage the Operational Area of Bank Branches: A Case Study.** Fundação Getúlio Vargas, Escola de Administração de Empresas de São Paulo, São Paulo, Brazil, November 2007. Published on <http://bibliotecadigital.fgv.br/dspace/bitstream/handle/10438/5852/112606.pdf?sequ ence=1>.

MACHADO, F.N.R. **Tecnologia e Projeto de Data Warehouse.** São Paulo: Erica, 2004.

MATTOS, Antonio C. M. **Sistemas de informação: uma visão executiva.** São Paulo: Saraiva, 2005.

MEINEM, Ênio; PORT, Márcio. **Credit Cooperatives yesterday, today and tomorrow.** Brasília: Confebras, 2012.

OLIVEIRA, Celso H. P. **SQL practical course.** São Paulo: Novatec Editora Ltda, 2002. ch.1, p.12.

OLIVEIRA, Douglas T.; PEREIRA, Otacilio J. **A study of Business Intelligence in the corporate environment.** 2008. Available at: <http://www.uw.br/edital_doc/UM%20ESTUDO%20DO%20BUSINESS%20INTELLI GENCE%20NO%20AMBIENTE%20EMPRESARIAL_6d7bdd4c-5bd5-447e-9c89- e247866a265f.pdf> Accessed on: 11 April 2014.

CREDIT CO-OPERATIVE PORTAL. **What is a credit union?** Available at: <http://cooperativismodecredito.coop.br/cooperativismo/o-   what-is-a-credit-cooperative/>. Accessed on: 16 June 2014.

Co-operativism. Available at   : <http://cooperativismodecredito.coop.br/cooperativismo/> Accessed on: 2 July 2014.

SANTOS, Maribel Yasmina; RAMOS, Isabel. **Business Intelligence: Information Technologies in Knowledge Management.** Lisbon: FCA-Editora de Informática, 2006.

SILVERS, F. **Building and Maintaining a Data Warehouse.** Boca Raton: Auerbach, 2008.

THOMPSON, **O. Business Intelligence Success, Lessons Learned.** Technology Evaluation Centres, October 9,   2004. Available at: < http://www.technologyevaluation.com/research/article/Business-Intelligence-Success-   Lessons-Learned.html>. Accessed on 28 October 2014.

TURBAN, Efraim; SHARDA, Ramesh; ARONSON, Jay; KING, David. **Business Intelligence - A Managerial Approach to Business Intelligence.** São Paulo: Person Education Inc, 2008.

ANNEX A - QUESTIONNAIRE

The importance of the analytical data environment (BI) in decision-making to leverage business in co-operatives

The aim of this survey is to assess your perception of the importance of the analytical data environment (BI) in decision making for business leverage at Sicoob cooperatives.

Mandatory

Which Business Unit do you work for? *

Identify the Business Unit in which you work.

Position *

Identify the position you hold in the Business Unit

How long have you worked in the Business Unit? *

Inform the length of time you have worked at Singular / Central / Bancoob / Confederation.

Level of Education *

Please state your level of education.

Sex*
Inform gender.

1 - Access to the analytical environment gives business managers greater autonomy in analysing and obtaining results *

	Concordo	Concordo Parcialmente	Discordo
Avaliação	○	○	○

2 - Analytical data allows managers to prospect for new business *

	Concordo	Concordo Parcialmente	Discordo
Avaliação	○	○	○

3 - There was a reduction in the data extraction process for generating product and service performance reports *

	Concordo	Concordo Parcialmente	Discordo
Avaliação	○	○	○

4 - The frequency with which analytical data is made available improves the business

management process *

	Concordo	Concordo Parcialmente	Discordo
Avaliação	C	C	C

5 - The analytical data provided enables a strategic view of the business *

	Concordo	Concordo Parcialmente	Discordo
Avaliação	C	C	C

6 - Implementations in the analytical environment will enable an integrated view of customers *

	Concordo	Concordo Parcialmente	Discordo
Avaliação	C	C	C

Printed by Books on Demand GmbH, Norderstedt / Germany